Mount Fuji

Rob Waring, *Series Editor*

T0052130

HEINLE
CENGAGE Learning™

Australia • Brazil • Japan • Korea • Mexico • Singapore • Spain • United Kingdom • United States

Words to Know

This story is set in the country of Japan. It's about a famous mountain there that is called Mount Fuji [fuʤi].

 Climbing Mount Fuji. Read the paragraph. Then match each word or phrase with the correct definition.

    Mount Fuji is an important symbol of Japan, both for Japanese people and international visitors. People can climb this famous mountain during a six-week period in July and August if there aren't any typhoons or other bad weather. So many people hike up the mountain that there are restaurants and vending machines that sell food and drinks at the top. In the summer, there are often festivals to celebrate the mountain. In fact, some people actually consider Mount Fuji to be a goddess.

1. symbol _____

2. typhoon _____

3. vending machine _____

4. festival _____

5. goddess _____

a. a machine from which people buy drinks and snacks

b. a female god

c. a bad ocean storm with very strong winds

d. a sign or object that represents something

e. a public celebration of a special occasion

Name: Mount Fuji
Japanese Name: *Fujisan*
Height: 3,776 meters (Japan's tallest mountain)
Best View: View from Shin Fuji Train Station

B A Religious Experience? Read the definitions. Then complete the paragraph with the correct form of the words.

pilgrimage: a journey to a place that has religious importance
worship: show respect for a god or gods by performing religious ceremonies
soul: the part of a person that is not physical and that some people believe continues to exist after death
spiritual: relating to strong feelings and beliefs, especially rellgious ones
purification: the process of making something clean and free from damaging substances

Originally, the purpose of climbing Mount Fuji was to make a religious (1)_____. At first, only men were allowed to climb the mountain as part of a (2)_____ process. They didn't want to clean their bodies; they wanted to clean their (3)_____. Today, anyone can climb the mountain, but for some, climbing it is a still (4)_____ experience. To these people, the mountain is like a goddess, and they want to (5)_____ her.

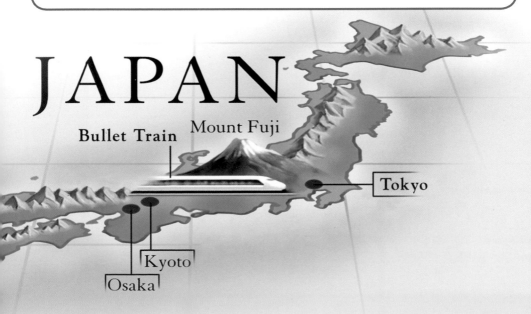

JAPAN

Bullet Train   Mount Fuji

Tokyo

Kyoto

Osaka

Karen Kasmauski[1], a National Geographic photographer, has traveled all the way from her home in the United States to the country of Japan. She has made the trip so that she can photograph one of the most significant symbols of Japanese culture: Mount Fuji.

It isn't going to be easy for Karen. It's raining hard and clouds cover the famous mountain. Karen only has a few days left before she must leave the country. She's starting to get a little bit nervous about the photography shoot. "I can't believe I'm looking for Fuji in the middle of a typhoon," she says. However, as she stands in the rain under an umbrella, you can tell that Karen hasn't lost hope completely. "I have three more days to go before I have to head back to the [United] States," she explains, "and hopefully between now and then I'll be able to see the mountain."

---

[1]**Kasmauski:** [kæsmauski]

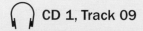 CD 1, Track 09

Skim for Gist

Read through the entire book quickly to answer the questions.

1. What's the reader basically about?

2. How do people generally feel about Mount Fuji?

Karen Kasmauski is a National Geographic photographer.

Finally, the rain stops and the beautiful view of Mount Fuji is clear again. Karen can climb the mountain and take photographs at last. She talks about why she thinks Mount Fuji is such an important mountain for Japanese people. She feels that it may be because it's very high, so it can be viewed from almost anywhere around it. She explains, "The mountain **dominates**[2] everything, and you can easily see how people would come to worship the mountain."

Another reason for Fuji's importance in Japanese culture is that some people feel that Mount Fuji is a goddess. Many festivals are held around the mountain to celebrate this 'goddess' Karen explains, "These festivals, called 'fire and water festivals,' are to sort of **appease**[3] the mountain ... [to] give celebration and gifts to the goddess Mount Fuji." She then adds, "[People do this] so that she will not destroy them."

---

[2]**dominate:** be the largest, most important, or most noticeable part of something
[3]**appease:** cause to feel better; please

Karen starts her photography shoot at the base of the mountain. This is where many of the main tourist attractions can be found. Mount Fuji attracts a huge number of tourists each year, and after a visit, most people want to go home with a gift. It's possible to buy almost anything with pictures of Fuji on it. As Karen talks about the tourist area, she mentions this fact. "You can have cookies, cakes, candies, **bento** boxes,[4] coffee cups, tea cups …" she explains, "whatever you can think of that you can put Fuji on—you'll find it."

Despite all of the buying and selling that goes on, for most Japanese people, climbing Mount Fuji still represents more than tourism. The challenge of climbing Fuji is in strengthening your body— and more importantly, your mind.

---

[4] **bento** box: a box of traditional Japanese food usually eaten as a meal

Karen finally starts hiking up the mountain, and it's not an easy climb. As she goes, she talks about how climbing it is actually more about the mind than the body. "Climbing Mount Fuji is a mind exercise. It's really **mind over matter**[5] more than anything," she says. "There's a word they use called *gambatte*, which is **'persevere'**.[6] 'Persevere' is a big word in Japanese culture and language." A person certainly needs to persevere in order to make such a long climb!

As Karen climbs, she stops from time to time to take photographs of the mountain and climbers. For her, it's a welcome break from the climb. She's also happy that it's not a hot, sunny day. She says, "I think it's good that it's a **misty**[7] day, because [the mist] has actually been able to cut down on the heat. Stopping to take pictures is a good excuse to take a break."

---

[5]**mind over matter:** using the mind to control the body in difficult times
[6]**persevere:** continue to try to do something although it is difficult
[7]**mist:** light, soft rain

Climbing Mount Fuji has been spiritually and religiously significant for a long time. Karen explains, "The original purpose of climbing Mount Fuji was a religious pilgrimage." Even today you will find people worshipping the mountain or other gods right in the middle of the noisy crowds and noodle shops at the top of Mount Fuji.

For climbers, it's often a very wonderful feeling to stand at the top of the mountain after a long climb and look at a beautiful sunrise. For Karen, the experience tends to be an emotional one as well. When she reaches the top, Karen expresses her thoughts, "I think it's always kind of an amazing event when you climb for 12 hours and you come up and see this **gorgeous**[8] sunrise. It just really is kind of an emotional event."

---

[8] **gorgeous:** beautiful; lovely

straw conical hat

tabi

Long ago, only men could climb Mount Fuji, and they often did it wearing straw conical hats and tabi.

These days, Mount Fuji is a very busy place that is full of climbers. When they get to the top, they're often thirsty, hungry, and ready to celebrate. There, climbers can buy food at small restaurants and drinks from vending machines. Japanese artists even sometimes perform music, and there are hundreds of people everywhere who are having a good time with their friends.

In the past, climbing Mount Fuji was different. Karen talks about what it was like to climb the mountain long ago. What kind of people climbed it and why? Karen explains: "The women were not allowed on the mountain until 1930, so these would be men climbing the mountain. [They] usually [climbed it] with '*tabis*,' which are these little white socks, and a white outfit with a **straw conical hat**."[9] She then adds, "People would climb on the mountain as a sort of a purification process of their soul."

---

[9]**straw conical hat:** a wide, round-based hat with sloping sides and a pointed top made from natural materials

Karen tries to summarize the experience of climbing Mount Fuji. She feels that it's an amazing adventure that's almost like an amusement park. She also feels that it's a national 'bonding experience', or an activity that brings the people of Japan closer together.

The top of the mountain is crowded with food stands and noisy waiters selling their foods. Karen talks about how all of this is possible. "There's a whole group of people who operate ... or who live on the mountain for about six to eight weeks at a time," she says. "[They] make this adventure possible for the 400,000 plus people that climb it during that six-week period," she adds. Karen then wonders about how all of this is done. "How do they get the food up there?" she says, "There [are] vending machines at the top of the mountain. How are the cans of soda brought to the top?" She then answers her own question, "Obviously, there's some vehicle that has to bring it to the top and it's the **bulldozer**."[10]

---

[10]**bulldozer:** a heavy, moving machine used to destroy buildings and make the ground level

Managing Mount Fuji during tourist season is a huge operation. At the end of the climbing season, there's still more work to do. "Toward the end of the season, they have a bunch of groups that come," she reports. "[They] clean up the mountain, because a lot of trash and **litter**[11] is left."

Karen explains that cleaning up the mountain is a kind of community duty for most of these people. Why? Because they are so proud of Mount Fuji and all that it represents. When one looks at beautiful Mount Fuji, it's easy to see the time and hard work that keeps it in good condition. It's also very easy to see that the effort is well worth it; Mount Fuji as beautiful as ever!

---

[11] **litter:** small pieces of trash on the ground

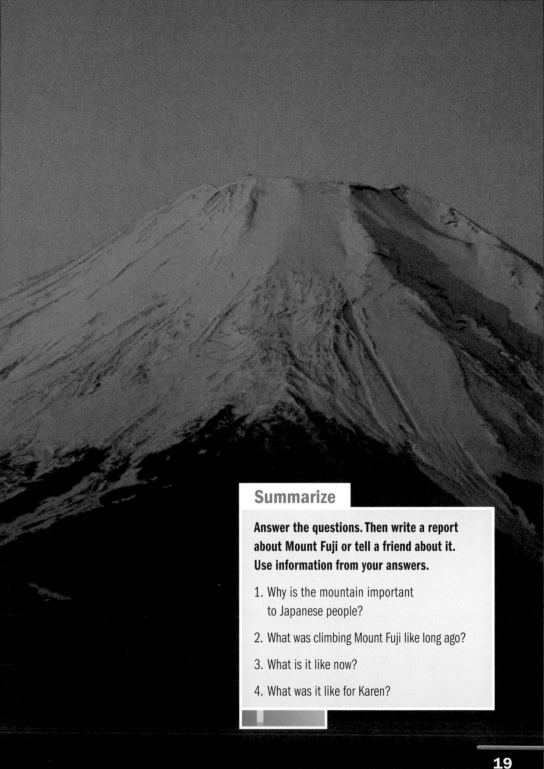

Summarize

Answer the questions. Then write a report about Mount Fuji or tell a friend about it. Use information from your answers.

1. Why is the mountain important to Japanese people?

2. What was climbing Mount Fuji like long ago?

3. What is it like now?

4. What was it like for Karen?

After You Read

1. Why does Karen Kasmauski visit Japan?
- **A.** to climb a mountain
- **B.** to experience a typhoon
- **C.** to take pictures
- **D.** to attend a festival

2. Karen is worried _____ the rain won't stop.
- **A.** about
- **B.** that
- **C.** if
- **D.** for

3. What's the purpose of the festivals on Mount Fuji?
- **A.** to protect people
- **B.** to please the mountain
- **C.** to celebrate the goddess
- **D.** all of the above

4. A suitable heading for paragraph 1 on page 8 is:
- **A.** Rare Mount Fuji Items
- **B.** No One Wants Cookies
- **C.** Mountain Images Hard to Find
- **D.** Plenty of Gift Choices

5. In paragraph 2 on page 8, the word 'represents' means:
- **A.** means
- **B.** presents
- **C.** introduces
- **D.** gives

6. What view about climbing Mount Fuji is expressed by Karen?
- **A.** Climbers need determination.
- **B.** A sunny day is best.
- **C.** Taking breaks is a bad idea.
- **D.** Climbers should speak Japanese.

7. In paragraph 1 on page 11, who is 'they'?
   A. climbers
   B. Japanese people
   C. tourists
   D. none of the above

8. In paragraph 1 on page 11, what does the word 'big' mean?
   A. large
   B. difficult
   C. important
   D. long

9. What kind of feeling does Karen have when she reaches the top?
   A. youthful
   B. amazement
   C. religious
   D. surprising

10. What has changed about climbing Mount Fuji from long ago?
    A. Fewer people climb now.
    B. People now wear traditional clothes.
    C. Anyone is allowed to try it now.
    D. Nothing has changed.

11. Which of the following is NOT a good heading for page 16?
    A. Difficulty Going Down
    B. Hikers Celebrate Together
    C. Operators Manage Everything
    D. Lively Mountain Top

12. What does the writer think about the Mount Fuji community?
    A. Their daily life is difficult.
    B. They don't like the tourists who litter.
    C. They care deeply for the mountain.
    D. They are tired at the end of hiking season.

High Adventure

Mountain climbing is an exciting adventure activity. For some, climbing is a spiritual journey—a type of pilgrimage to the heart of nature, and a cleansing of the soul. For others, the physical challenge is more important. The mountain becomes a symbol of their ability to achieve a difficult goal through perseverance. People climb thousands of mountains each year, but the following are some of the most popular sites:

KILIMANJARO

Some people say that Mount Kilimanjaro, the tallest mountain in Africa, is one of the easiest mountains to climb. Tourists regularly do it with little more than a walking stick and proper clothing. One amazing aspect of the trip is the changes in climate that occur. At the bottom, everything is warm and green. Higher up, climbers enter thick forests before they move into a wide area with very few trees and plants. Finally, the top of Kilimanjaro is covered with snow.

ACONCAGUA

Mount Aconcagua, Argentina, is the highest mountain in the Americas and one of the highest in the world. Climbers can take up to 12 days to reach the top. They generally stop about halfway up the mountain at Plaza de Mulas. They may stay there for several days while their bodies get used to being up so high. Weather conditions on the trip vary from snow and wind to blue skies and sun. The return trip is usually much faster, sometimes it lasts only two days.

Three Popular Mountains to Climb				
Mountain	Height in Meters	Attempted Climbs in a Typical Year	Successful Climbs in a Typical Year	Typical Success Rate
Kilimanjaro	5,895	25,000–30,000	12,000–15,000	40–50%
Aconcagua	6,960	3,300–3500	900–1,000	27–30%
Mt. Everest	8,850	500–600	125–150	25–33%

MOUNT EVEREST

Mount Everest is one of the tallest mountains in the world, and it's also one of the most dangerous to climb. Temperatures are well below zero and the winds can be as strong as 160 kilometers per hour. Every year, people die during attempted climbs. About one in five people who reach the top do not survive the trip back down. Here are some very special people who made successful climbs:

- The first woman to reach the top was Junko Tabei in 1975.
- The oldest person was Yuichiro Miura in 2003. He was 70 years old.
- The youngest person was Temba Tsheri in 2001. He was 15 at the time.

CD 1, Track 10

Word Count: 355
Time: _____

23

Vocabulary List

appease (7)
bento **box** (8)
bulldozer (16)
dominate (7)
festival (2, 7)
goddess (2, 3, 7)
gorgeous (12)
litter (18)
mind over matter (11)
mist (11)
persevere (11)
pilgrimage (3, 12)
purification (3, 15)
soul (3, 15)
spiritual (3, 12)
straw conical hat (14, 15)
symbol (2, 4)
typhoon (2, 4)
vending machine (2, 15, 16)
worship (3, 7, 12)